About the

Mary was born in Australia, lived in Malta and finally moved to the UK, over twenty years ago, where she currently lives.

She has kept a journal of her thoughts and life experiences since the age of sixteen. Her other publication, *Liberation at Long Last,* by M. Mallia (XLibris © 2014), is a touching semi-autobiographical account, in novel form, of her inner journey alongside that of her mother's, inspired by her late mother's brutal suicide twenty years earlier. It depicts how despair and death are triumphantly overcome by love, faith and letting go.

Mary's love of poetry can be traced back to her secondary school days, but she only started writing poetry herself in the last four years. *A Return to*

Love to the Heart of God (Pegasus © 2021) is the first book of poetry Mary has published. It depicts the journey from brokenness to wholeness as one rediscovers the connection to the divine universe, infinite Life, Love, Light, reverberating within the sacred, pure cosmic sound.

THE PLAYING FIELDS

MARY M.

THE PLAYING FIELDS

Vanguard Press

VANGUARD PAPERBACK

© Copyright 2021
Mary M.

The right of Mary M. to be identified as author of
this work has been asserted by her in accordance with the
Copyright, Designs and Patents Act 1988.

A CIP catalogue record for this title is
available from the British Library.

ISBN 978 1 80016 178 8

*Vanguard Press is an imprint of
Pegasus Elliot MacKenzie Publishers Ltd.*
www.pegasuspublishers.com

First Published in 2021

Vanguard Press
Sheraton House Castle Park
Cambridge England
Printed & Bound in Great Britain

Dedication

To my two sons, Matthew and Daniel, who have been the pinnacle of my life as it has played out in my own personal *Playing Fields*. They unleashed a love within me I didn't even know I had.

Acknowledgements

I would like to thank my two sons, Matthew and Daniel, who have been very good playmates as well as great teachers. I have always believed that there is a lot that I must learn from them and that it is they who shall teach me much more than I can ever teach them.

I am grateful to Superjur (SDC) Mr Victor Delicata for having been a great spiritual teacher and father to me since the ages of fourteen to twenty. He showed great faith in me and great respect as a spiritual being of light and as a teacher. May his soul rest in peace.

Thanks to my father, Carmelo, who has always encouraged me to follow my dreams. He has always been proud of me doing so.

Thanks go to my A level economics private tuition teacher, Mr Ernest Azzopardi, who never gave up on me in my lack of understanding and attention to detail. I will always remember his generosity with heartfelt gratitude, as getting that piece of paper opened so many other doors which would've otherwise been shut.

I would also like to thank, Dr Ronald Sultana, who as an inspiring teacher in secondary school, was the first to get me thinking outside the box. He then followed up his good work at university during my B.Ed (Hons.) degree, with his perception-changing course in critical thinking. This taught me to question narratives no matter who writes them, usually the ones whom they serve do, anyway! As my dissertation tutor he taught me to observe keenly and analyse objectively.

I am indebted to my Yoga, Meditation and Pranayama teacher, Mr Maarten Vermaase, for having dedicated his whole life passing onto all his students, including myself, a wealth of life-changing knowledge and wisdom transmitted from his own teachers to himself, humbly and sincerely unto us.

I am whole-heartedly grateful to the whole team at Pegasus, for believing in my writing, and realising my dream of publishing my poems, come true. Thank you.

To all my friends throughout the whole of my life whether they have found themselves in this collection of poems or not, with whom I have shared life experiences, friendship, fun and frolics for all of whom I am truly grateful.

Each in your own unique way has contributed something to what, where and who I am today.

With heartfelt gratitude,
Mary

Contents

Introduction

This collection of poetry, varying from simple light-hearted children's sing-song rhymes to some deeply profound, thought-provoking verses, are intended to challenge as well as to entertain.

In the first volume, *The Children*, we encounter the protagonists as some skilfully perform and others joyfully play. Their value — inherent in being Divine — is not defined by their achievements, talents or skills. Each partakes of the Divine One infinite and eternal Cosmic Conscious tapestry of Love, Life and Light reverberating within sacred, cosmic sound — and is a unique expression of it.

The Playing Fields is the setting within which all the children perform, and or play. It had been created immaculately flawless. Everything in it had been finely balanced and ran in perfect unison and harmony. Hearts were soft, spacious, all-embracing, non-judgemental, generous, kind, loving, compassionate… Minds were free, open, wise, discerning, seeing… Bodies were strong, healthy, supple and free from disease. All expressed their uniqueness in a way that respected everybody else's — it couldn't be any other way. Nobody's expression was better than another's, nobody's work less valuable than any other's. There was no anger, anguish, agony, shame, fear, guilt, greed, lust, jealousy, control, coercion, manipulation, lies, deceit, poverty, injustice, illness or death.

Until *The Fall* or *The Split* happened.

Who caused it, how and why, isn't as important as much as the destruction and devastation it has procured throughout history to this very day. In *The End Game* it is perceived as the ongoing battle of Evil against Good; Demons against Humanity; Dark against Light; Sin against Grace; the realms of Hell against Heavenly realms. It is pertinent that the forces of darkness and evil are overthrown should humanity choose to walk the Earth in peace, love and joy as had always been intended.

Those who rediscover and reconnect to those innate child-like qualities within them which they enjoyed probably until the ages of about six, seven, eight or nine, shall inherit the Earth… finding the audacity to see the world as if for the first time… rediscovering a sense of curiosity… wonder… awe… the courage to fight for the freedom to play one's own games… the voice to speak out one's own truth without worrying what others might think… or say… simple honesty… simplicity… authenticity… living in the present moment… not holding onto anger… not being hankered by fear… but embraced by boundless, loving energy…

believing all is possible, because it is, in the divine, infinite realm of boundless possibility!

Humanity's playgrounds and playing fields have become a hellish place to play. Will Humanity see how everybody's innocence, freedom and fun are being destroyed? Will they call upon their own Divinity to save a fallen Humanity? Will new playing fields and playgrounds be manifested in time, through its visionaries who dare to dream a new dream creating a new reality for Humanity? One in which a lost innocence is reclaimed, restoring the Earth to its original state — as had always been God's dream, I mean!

What if Humanity chooses not to?

VOLUME I — THE CHILDREN

"Are you coming out to play later today?"
We always used to ask each other every day
after school
that used to be so cool.

Lovers in the Flesh

I suddenly hear a knock at the door
and a shuffle in the garden, what's more.
Who is it at this ungodly time
Who disturbs my evening fine?

The second knock is louder still
I wait behind the door until
there is a silent space
and I shout just in case

My visitor is deaf! For,
the knocks at the door
sounded very loud and urgent
I ask: "Who is it, lady or gent?"

The reply comes in a gentle laugh
sounding like a smirk and a half!
Slowly I open the front door.
Looking like never before
stood before me a tall, smart man,
"Guess who I am, if you can!"

Was I asleep or was I awake,
I couldn't tell for goodness sake!
This gentleman did familiar seem

but, I still wasn't sure if this were a dream.
The man I did recognise tall and smart
cheeky, sensuous glances at him I dart.
As if reading my mind
he came in from behind
the plant that stood in the hallway,
"I'd love to come in, if I may."

"You are already in," I replied,
as a deep excited sigh, I sighed.
I ask if we'd ever met.
"Yes," came the reply, "on a TV set.
You played the Virgin fine,
I pretended you were mine.
Do you remember this incident
which I'm sure wasn't an accident?"

I looked at the gentleman standing before me
trying to get some sort of clarity.
My mind befuddled,
my body muddled
as this man they could not recall,
although very handsome and tall.

He moved towards me
slowly and seductively.
Was this the part we had played,
were love and passion displayed?
He looked tender and compassionate

peaceful, loving and rather passionate.
We hugged and kissed
my lips he just missed,
so we brushed cheek against cheek
I could start feeling my knees go weak
as he continued to come closer to me
I wondered what his next step would be!

My heart fluttered
as my mouth muttered
a few sweet nothings in his ear
I shouted, so he could hear!

Still not sure if awake or asleep
does here Illusion, Reality meet?
What will be his next move
would it his identity prove?

Should I have let a stranger come in
to my house, just on an impulsive whim?
He does seem strangely familiar so,
I decided to go with the flow.

My heart likes his vibration warm
my mind, my heart tries to warn:
"Are you sure this is what you desire,
he does seem to be wildly on fire?"

My heart reassures my mind,

it does him very handsome find
and since the feeling is mutual
I perform the forthcoming ritual.

A long red silken sari I wear
I've had it a long time, I swear!
He unwraps me carefully and lovingly
little by little my bare body he can see.

Little bits appearing slowly one at a time.
Intrigued he remarks: "Your skin it does shine
and smells of sweet-smelling fragrant flowers
refreshing as fresh April showers."

I coyly look into his ocean blue eyes
and say what he said was very nice!
Slowly I slide onto the beckoning bed
and from here onwards enough's been said!
Our bodies entwined and smouldering with heat
moving as one from our head to our feet
we rumbled
and tumbled
with total abandon
an act so seemingly random!

His slow languid kiss melted all my fears
His gentle caress moved me to tears.
Is this man human or from another dimension?
His touch so light, I forgot to mention.

It made me wonder whence he had come
and how so suddenly we seemed to be one.
How can I explain how he made me feel,
still asking myself if this is really for real.
Is he a man or an angel Divine
is this reality or a dream of mine?

His touch came as light as a feather
caressing me all over and whether
it was a dream or not,
my whole being was very hot!

In his gentle embrace
tension melted
bodies sweltered
hearts sheltered
souls expanding
beings spacious
sounds explicit
consent implicit
passions flying
fears dying
abandoning to the present
spirits upward ascend
heavenly roses scent
like a sweet perfume
filling the entire room.

And suddenly he is there no more!

Had he bolted for the door?
This new union — being as one
ended before it'd even begun!

On the floor he left a tiny white feather
awake, asleep, man, angel whether.
He left as suddenly as he had come
bereft my body feels like a half, not one!
How could he so suddenly go?
That's what I really wanted to know!

The feather softly whispered in my ear:
"He isn't gone, dear, he's very near!"
I looked around and couldn't see
where he had taken himself to be.
I feel a freshly blowing breeze
and suddenly I begin to sneeze.
I come into the room with a bump
and fall onto the floor with a thump.
The feather I pick up from the floor
as the dream, is a dream no more!

Lovers in Spirit

Are you here, my darling,
in Spirit and in Truth?
I am your presence awaiting
your dearest, darling Ruth.

I am here waiting, Ruth,
my dearest darling sweet'art
can't wait to hold you in my arms
and off into my warm heart cart.

My dearest, darling David,
I have waited for so long
to dance embraced in your sweet caress
as our bodies dance our song.

My sweetest, darling, sweetheart Ruth,
my being for you languidly longs
to be caressed by your smooth skin's
like being touched, by Heavenly throngs.

My dearest, darling David,
can you hear my being pine,
then as you gently approach me
it suddenly begins to shine?

My sweetest, darling Sweetheart,

my old heart skips a beat
when your elusive image in dreams
comes to me in my sleep.

My dearest, darling David,
I hope I do not shock.
When I come to you in your dreams
I hope me you do not block.

Oh gentlest, sweetest, darling Ruth,
I await these visions sweet
I cannot contain myself with joy,
with the anticipation of when we meet.

Oh, dearest, darling David,
I am gladly reassured
that our meeting has been planned
soon, by the Heavens procured.

Oh, dearest, darling David,
I do not intend to tease
our real encounter on the Earth plane
I must ASAP release!

Oh, sweetest, gentlest, darling Ruth,
"How can this come to be?
How can you make dreams come true?"
I humbly ask of thee.

Oh, dearest darling, David,
it's all been written down
take heart and do not be sad,
quickly wipe away that frown.

Oh, sweetest, gentlest, darling Ruth,
I am so very happy
that one day very soon
you shall come to me.

Oh, dearest, darling David,
it's the other way around.
I heard through the grapevine
I will need to be found.

Oh, sweetest, gentlest, darling Ruth,
where do I begin
to look for thee throughout the Earth
without and wherein?

Oh, dearest, darling David,
make sure you follow your nose
it's not a very small one
and great at smelling, I suppose!

Oh, sweetest, gentlest, darling Ruth,
isn't that a bit rude?
Would you tease me with my nose
isn't that rather crude?

I imagine you like an angel
swanning in the air —
remarking on the size of my nose
I don't think that that's fair!

Oh, dearest, darling David,
I don't mean to be mean,
I do like teasing quite a bit
not meaning to demean.

Oh, sweetest, gentlest, darling Ruth,
I might be tall and handsome
but to lift you up sky-high
I might demand a ransom.

Oh, dearest, darling David,
what if I offer you my heart?
What if my love, affection
and respect in your life play a part?

Is that enough a ransom
offered in exchange, for
being lifted up so high
I can't offer any more.

Oh, sweetest, sweetheart Ruth,
what more can I expect?
That makes me a happy man

your heart and love, I will protect.

You won't just reach the cupboard
or get something from up the loft.
I shall lift you up inside yourself
our bodies and hearts squidgy soft!

This lifting up business
to the heavens and above
akin to flying in the spirit
soaring spirits in Love.

And just before we meet in spirit
I hope we meet in the flesh.
I look forward to our encounter
the anticipation of it, I relish.

Oh, dearest, darling David,
this dream is nearing its end.
Will you to my expectant heart
a little message, sign and send?

Pepsi I

A little black cat
came and sat
on my sofa
on my bed.

"Who are you?" I asked,
as in your warmth I basked.
"What is your name?
You just came
out of nowhere
it seems
like in dreams.
Are you real and true
feels like I've always known you."

The little black cat
as it sat
on my sofa
on my bed
on my lap
made itself at home
for a while.
My Loneliness smiled
as it came inside
warming my house
with its love.

Then it suddenly departed.
I suddenly started
to feel cold again.

The next day, it purred outside my door
Its paws pressing against the cold floor.
I quickly ushered it inside
from the cruel world to hide.
"You're always welcome here, my dear,"
I whispered softly in its bloody chewed ear.

Had it been in a fight,
come to me in flight
for shelter
from the cold
outside
had he come here to hide?

We play, we cuddle and we kiss
as its affection I might miss
I put all chores to one side
and allow him to sit beside
me, as I write
and busily type
a verse or two
about you,
Pepsi.

For in my enquiries

as answer to my queries
I am told your name is 'Pepsi'
You are male they say, verily!

So a male black cat
called 'Pepsi'
's been visiting me
almost every day
come what may.
Sometimes he would miss a day or two
but, that's OK for I knew
in time he would come back
and purr outside my front door
wanting a cuddle and what's more
a little affection and a play
easing the loneliness of the day.
My days are lonely no more
since he's been miaowing at my door.
I look forward in anticipation
to his purrs
and fluffy tail
moulting all over
the floor
the sofa
the bed
my lap.

Pepsi, my faithful and constant friend
changed my world in an instant.

The moment he knocked at my door
I wasn't lonely any more.
A new lease on life he has given me
I am as happy as can be!

My days are turned upside down,
Pepsi wiped away every frown
put a smile on my sad face
as if I were full of grace.
Was he that powerful a cat
that my mood he changed
sadness exchanged
for joy in my bones
like stepping stones
to the heavens fill me
with heavenly glee?

I call the cat by another name
I hope it doesn't mind.
Pepsi it turns out,
I shall whisper and not shout
is female and not male!
Does his-her owner know
the cat they've called Pepsi
is a female cat?
Has she ever sat
on their lap
for a nap?

Or on their bed
joyfully curled
and peacefully purred
caressing her fluff
calling 'his' bluff?

For he is a she
couldn't they see?
They had known her much longer than me!
I only had her roll onto her back
when I knew amidst her black
fur, it was tits I saw
and not a willie.
How could they have been so silly?

Pepsi II

Pepsi

I got suddenly and rudely taken
my warmth and comfort crudely shaken!
Why was Mary picking me up,
and handing me to that woman who wouldn't shut
up?
To a woman who loves me not, she handed me
over, to a woman with whom I didn't want to be.

For to her a beast I am, a pest!
No feelings, thoughts or at best
a sentient being with no rights,
always getting into fights
which I was not, of course,
that is all a lie, so false!

Her big dog called Belle
is not. It's really a hell
of a beastly carnivorous canine
whose outward countenance is benign.
However, deep inside, its wrath
seeks to make me into a broth!

My ears she chews
and my chin too.

My eyes she grazes,
to mention but a few
of the injuries she inflicts
intentionally to hurt and scar
growling, I hear her from afar.
I have to seek refuge elsewhere
I stay nearby, I don't go too far.

This youngish, friendly new lady I seek
I remember the first time we did meet.
She called to me from by the pavement
I went to her and made a clear statement
that overwhelmingly pleased to see her I was
as I rolled on my belly and purred, I suppose!

I remember when I saw her that very first time
it seemed as if she had been an owner of mine.
Perhaps, in another life, another setting
I lay on my back and enjoyed her gentle petting
as she stroked me and whispered words sweet and
kind.
Wow, it was amazing, do you think I did mind?
No, I was overwhelmingly over the moon
that my prayers will be answered soon.
I should be able to go to her homely house
there I shall stay, lay as quiet as a mouse.
I promised her I won't be any trouble at all
there I shall take refuge, life will be a ball!
As Mary is a kind-hearted loving soul

on whom life has sadly taken its toll,
welcomed me into her life with joy
as if to her a brand-new toy
to play with, and have some fun
a new life for her and I, had now begun.

A friendship ensued
but now all's being reviewed!
As I end up back in my owners' abode
I am not happy, it must be emphatically told!
They locked me up in a very tiny cage
my owner and her husband overflowing with rage
at me having sought out my own sanctuary,
to them an enraging outrageous travesty.

How dare *their* cat fight for its right
to seek its own owner and for this right fight?
How dare *their* cat whose sex they did not know,
its love and affection on another bestow?
How dare *their* pet which they neglected be set
on being adopted by a stranger? This they won't let
happen, not over their dead bodies they swore
as a demeanour ferocious and vicious they wore.

I have to find a way, Mary to warn
for her they regard with the greatest of scorn.
They definitely do not wish her well
this to her promptly I need to tell.
They are keeping me locked inside

but, here inside I shall not hide.
I shall find a way to escape soon
to go and tell Mary about this doom.
Mary must be waiting worriedly for me
and will worry when me she does not see!
She must have got my bowl of food ready
wet food, dried food and water for my brekkie!
She must be calling my name out loud
but, outside at this mo' I am not allowed.
I shall have to find a way Mary to tell,
But how, I am locked up in a cold prison cell?
She must come and rescue me very soon I hope
otherwise, with this enslavement I might not cope,
without the love of my sweet, sweet Mary
who I know is quite often, quite contrary!

My ardent prayer to God Divine
is being back with my Mary where all's fine,
returning to the comfort of her house
where I shall be as quiet as a mouse.

Mary

"Pepsi, Pepsi, I am so sorry
I am weary and sick with worry
as I carried you to her who is not nice
my apologies alone will not suffice.
I shall have to find a way to set you free
from her evil tyranny!

I can hear you miaowing as if by my door
I open, and there you are no more!
I look at the gate,
at half past eight
You are not there
I wait, stop and stare.
Hoping you've been set free
running back gleefully to me.

But, so far you have not.
Guilt inside me does rot
inside it does ferment
although I did put up a fight and an argument
making clear my outright view and sentiment
that I did not want to let you outside, in the cold
stay
and that in my house you're welcome any day.
She did not like my assertive stance.
She kept you locked up inside creating distance.
She was arrogant and angry when she came to
collect you
threatening that me she shall shortly sue
for sheltering you and loving you.
A note of these things I made
as farewell, her I bade.
She said repeatedly you were *her* cat
it doesn't seem like it, from where I'm sat!

You chose to come to me
to share good times and company.
Our times always full of cheerful chatter
it seems like nothing else does matter.
I tried to get you some good food to eat
as your tummy rumbled, it needed meat
and some other food to nourish your being,
as clusters of fur on the floor I was seeing.

I feel very guilty as I should've let her shout
for you from your refuge to slowly come out.
I shouldn't have so simply handed you to her
so sorry that to have done. And as I err,
I also ask for forgiveness of you
do you think this you can give to me to
ease my guilt and sense of shame
as I feel I'm slowly losing this game?

Pepsi

When she came to collect me
She was very arrogant and rude
I heard her hoarse harsh command.
How could she have been so crude?

Threatening to sue you is what she does best
as her little cat Pepsi flees the nasty nest
and seeks safety elsewhere.
She thinks: "How does he dare?"

She thinks that because me she occasionally feeds
and to own and control me she avidly needs,
that I belong to her and her family.
Do I want to be a part of her tyranny?

No, I do not! And on that note, I say
Her and her soul-destroying edicts I shall not obey!
Her desire to control, consume and destroy me,
is evident for you and everybody else to see!

I shall find a way out of this imprisonment
to everybody's shock, horror, astonishment!
As a very powerful and creative cat am I
I shan't take it lying down and die!
I shall fight for my freedom with all my zeal
and when I do, as I will do for real,
I shall make sure she knows I set myself free
as I scratch the sofa and all her bedding with glee.
I shall not hover and hanker about
but, swiftly come to your door and shout:

"Mary, Mary,
Quite contrary
do not worry, do not fret
One thing do not forget!
There is nothing to forgive
for as long as I shall live
I shall remember your kindness and generosity too
I know you love me and I will always love you!"

Two Black Cats

A blue velvet sofa I used to own
Two black cats sit on this stately throne.
Their furry bodies warm the seat
as their bottom the seat's bottom meet.

They sit languidly whilst I hustle and bustle.
Rosie intently looks at leaves as they rustle,
but stays inside in the warmth of the room
whilst herself she zealously does groom.

Matey on the other hand loves the outdoors,
prowling outside fighting territory wars.
She firmly stands her ground
walking stealthily around.

Hunting down the odd bird or two,
a present for me, which I misconstrue
for a being has been suddenly shaken
as its poor life is unsuspectingly taken

Given to me as a gift from Matey
in great reverence and generosity.
Rosie would join in the fun
chasing until that battle's won.

Playing copycats

catching rats
dancing about
silently shout
sleeping peacefully
walking gleefully
eating hungrily
playing merrily.

Oh, I wish, I wish I were a cat
sitting snugly on a warm soft mat.
Unaware of trouble, toil and strife
oblivious to all of life's dreadful
illnesses, deaths and blinding illusions
sleeping peacefully through fatal delusions.

Gareth and David Icke

Dearest Gareth Icke
I very simply like
the way you are open to Spirit
Its Consciousness without any limit
is able to flood through you
throughout your being imbue
Words of wisdom that rhyme
and a Love Infinite, a Love Divine.

(As a thanksgiving to Gareth for all his work and
speech some of it rapped, in Trafalgar Square,
London on Saturday 26th September 2020)

Dearest David Icke
I very simply like
the power of your words so strong
outlining all that's sadly wrong
in our world today
broken-heartedly, I say!

Your message, one of Hope
giving people's' life a scope.
Outlining how to stop this madness
amidst the chaos and all the sadness.
Your life of Truth a testimony
of Consciousness' Infinite Divinity.

(As a thanksgiving to David for all his work and inspiring speech in Trafalgar Square, London on Saturday 26th September 2020)

Written by Mary for Gareth and David Icke on Saturday 3rd October 8:15am.

Angela and Mary

I stopped to speak to Angela
on my way back from my walk.
We warmly exchanged greetings
as the robin nearby began to talk:

"Dearest Angela and Mary
you are both, so dear
it's nice to stop for a chat
that's why I'm stopping here.

I love to see you both smile
as you greet each other now.
Oh, how I love it when you
humans connect — it's wow!

For I know you only met
one other time before.
Mary you were walking past
Angela you were by your door.

It was a hasty meeting
there was lots of commotion,
Today's calm connection
set a new friendship in motion.

It's just so lovely and refreshing
to watch humans smile.
Things are getting pretty hefty
I can't imagine why!

Creation from my point of view
has always been so perfect.
The laws that bind us all in Love
in our hearts do reflect

The love of our Creator
The Father's work of art
is our Creation not perfect,
Oh Life, where do I start?

It seems as if the arms of Death
have stretched across the Earth
filled its people with its Darkness,
Do they not know their worth?"

The Little Robin Red-Breast

I'm a little red-breast robin
I know perfectly who I am.
I instinctively sing my heart out
as is Love's very own plan.

I bring so much soul solace
to people fumbling in the Dark.
Yet, I am not much to look at,
people my presence do hark.

Especially at Christmas time
That very special time of year,
My image on many Christmas cards
They do hold me so dear.

Perhaps, as I abide by laws
of Nature so good and true
it doesn't matter what I look like
it just does — that I love you!

My song from my heart is ushered
filling my lungs and chest
and all the space for miles around me
north, south, east and west.

My greys sometimes do get me down
Yet, my red I always wear with pride.
All-in-all I am a robin red-breast
and my true colours, I do not hide.

You couldn't see the red as clearly
if the grey feathers weren't there.
The grey isn't always celebrated
I don't think that that's fair.

Doris and Helen

My Dearest sister Helen,
and my sister Doris too
time has not erased,
the love I have for you.

My Dearest sister Helen,
and my sister Doris too
you are always in my heart,
whatever you say or do.

My Dearest sister Helen,
and my sister Doris too
Our paths cross now once again,
Oh, how I have missed you!

Your dearest sister Mary
had not gone away
you wouldn't get rid of her so easily,
she is in your life to stay.

Mary, Mary quite contrary
that's how she's always been.
She loves you both forever more
this can now be clearly seen.

Her life we know's been tricky

Her suffering's been great,
to meet up with you both one day
she can hardly wait!
No end to her agonised anguish
or to her endless poignant pain.
Yet, one day you all shall meet up
come wind, hail, snow or rain.
And when you three all get together
Oh, how the Heavens shall ring.
Everybody shall be able to hear,
Angelic choirs of angels sing.

They're singing of a reuniting
Of Heaven's a simple soul,
Here on Earth sojourning
spreading peace and love their goal.

As you reunite in friendship,
so do your Life paths merge
and once again the power of love
between you will emerge.

You do not need to meet in body
in spirit, that'll be fine.
For when the good Lord comes, He says:
"Come on! You three are mine.

The Enemy tried to destroy
What I had so diligently planned

He did his best to undo my work
He can't! This he has learnt.

I gather back my three, little sheep
back in the fold together they come.
I do not have a favourite amongst them
for to me they are unique, yet one.

Each in their way uniquely made
Each their life-purpose living out
yet, when the marching order comes
the three in unison shall begin to shout:

"We love our God with all our might,
our Saviour and our Lord.
Whatever life does throw at us
whether peace, harmony or discord,
our faith stays unshakeably strong
in our God and His Heavenly throng.
For each in our own little way
to Love, we humbly pray
that God's will be done unto us
without too much fuss.
We ask that God's will be fulfilled
as it is by Divine Life, Love, Light, willed.

It seems we have been separate
Yet, the whole time we've been apart
God has held each of us in Love's bosom
safely, in the centre of Love's loving heart.

There we are not separate,
there we are all one.
In and by Love Divine
all battles shall be won.

Lindzi

Lindzi, Lindzi, Lindzi, Lindzi,
some would say she's rather flimsy!
They haven't heard her lioness' roar
seen her courage and much much more.

She is risen from the ashes,
like a phoenix standing tall.
She now knows her true value
and doesn't feel small any more.

When you have Lindzi as your friend
with everything under the sun, you can contend
as she protects all those who are near
with a vengeance, not fear!

This Lindzi's a treasure of infinite worth
to endless works of art, she gives birth.
For what her eyes see, her hands can make
giving new life to lifeless matter, a new shape.

Co-creator with our Maker Divine
from nothing she calls forth patterns sublime,
transforming raw material into being
you might not believe, without seeing.

Within the spot on her forehead
what is commonly called the "Third Eye"
sharp, colourful, clairvoyant images
adorn her vision like a clear blue sky.

The pictures on this canvas clear
always give a message, my Dear
to those seeking an answer or two,
it could be me, or it could be you!

Lindzi, Lindzi, Lindzi, Lindzi,
although perceived by some as rather flimsy
is actually made of strength
and would go to any length
to defend her beloved ones
whom she loves tons and tons.

A courage she has now procured
in the face of evil, steadily secured,
A defiance to what is wrong,
despite persecution, still singing her song.
A tune of sweet-smelling perfume
whose scent mystifies the room.

Truth is her alibi and always has been.
She has the ability to see what can't be seen
by the naked human eye,
as in the Spirit realm it doth lie.
A treasure so true
with gratitude, I thank you.

Anna and Aileen

My dearest sister Anna
that compassionate, gentle smile
brings solace to your friends
all the while… all the while!

My dearest sister Aileen
I love it when you call.
I relish our conversations
about the big things and the small.

My dearest sister Anna
so sincere and so true
sharing an honest friendship with you
I am well and truly grateful.

My dearest sister Aileen
I love it when you smile
especially when on long walks we go
mile, after mile after mile!

My dearest sister Anna
the roads from Russia to here
miles and miles away
brought us somehow together, Dear.

My dearest sister Aileen

it's strange how our paths met.
Bumping 'coincidently' in Waitrose,
seems like it had been somehow set.

Back to your homeland
you took my beloved son.
He loved it there each mo' and day
having had such great fun.

Both friendships steadfast through the years
through life's inevitable ups and downs,
changing moods, discussing foods
transforming into smiles life's frowns.

My dearest sister Aileen
I just want to say today
I shall always hold you dear in my heart
come what may, come what may!

Your garden so pristinely pruned,
Anya, sunflowers smiling in the sun.
Finally, on this note I'd love to say
these friendships 're second to none!

Lara

Her name is not Sara, or not even Clara.
No! Her beautiful name is simply, Lara.
I met her one sunny day on a walk
out of the blue, we began to talk.

I love her purity
shrouded so subtly
in her talk grounded in reality.
I could feel in me Spirit stir,
there where we were!

Unpretentious and humble is she
leaving a lot of peace with me
as she walked away
slowly at the end of the day.

As we chatted on that very first day,
we both had had a lot to say.
Her — wondering what to do for the best
Me — talking of miracles and all the rest
Her — gently softly spoken
Me — coarse, yet heart wide open
Her — tall, slim, slender and very kind
Me — shorter and stumpier you will find
Her — full of poise and grace
Me — probably with food on my face!

Her — silken, long, straight hair
Me — curls blowing everywhere.

Since then, this friendship grew
as that shoot that day was planted new.
The tree has been generous and kind
yielding juicy, delicious fruits you will find.

Children@school
(October 2018 – December 2019)

She told me: "We've been waiting for you."
I stupidly didn't dare ask: "Who?"
For deep inside I hoped for the best,
Didn't see it as the penultimate test!

Satan and his Hell
awaiting the knell
of my love ringing
my joy singing
of grace and compassion
embracing my mission
to bring to this Hell
of Heaven the knell.

I stayed in that hell
my soul ringing, its knell
melted away hard-hearts
threw Cupid's love darts
scored a bull's eye
in their hearts and my
Grace shone bright.
Oh, what a happy sight!
Heaven smiles sweet
Where evil and Grace meet.
Heaven's rejoicing now

as demons to Love bow.
The former melt
in a sweaty swelt
sweet-smelling of Love and Light
shining, shimmering, dazzling bright.
Hearts opened wide
front, back and side.

The boss was not pleased!
"She must be released
from her duty of care
she loves too much. How does she dare
to melt boundaries and heal division
to embody and manifest the Heavenly vision?

She now has to go
as she must know.
I AM BOSS!
It's not our loss!
She mustn't stay,
evil hearts sway."

Heaven decreed
and all agreed,
she would soon have to leave
but all agree and all believe
that Hell was hell once more,
the moment she walked out that door!

P.S. The 'She' in the few verses above…

She now teaches a class called Green.
Often you can hear her scream
Shouting out loud, at everybody one and all
as she stands surreptitiously straight and tall.
Harsh commands she bellows out
and if the students are about,
to argue or if they dare to disobey
she admonishes harshly: "Stop! I say.
I'm in control, complete control.
I decide how the dice doth roll.
I decide what you can consume
and when playtime will resume.
The establishment doth me employ
for all your souls to simply destroy."

Her fate is currently undecided
as Life her has harshly chided,
showing her the error of her ways
as precepts of darkness, she obeys.

To Gabriel
The Fallen Archangel

I don't need a recording to tell me
anything that I don't know already.
I'm not saying this through pride
but, with the greatest humility
as Love's servant here to serve and restore
Humanity as before the split,
May Love's will be done, our light lit.

As we are all Sacred and Divine
we all our inner voice must find.
It is not on a tape recorder or on YouTube.
It beats in our own heart
shines in and through our being
A gift so great
A gift sublime
A gift truly sacred, Divine.

Inside us like a little rhyme
is Love's voice speaking unto us
Quietly, gently without any fuss.
Those who listen, know It's voice
when they hear it, they have a choice —
to give over their power to the Dark force
or — to heed the Love in their hearts, of course!

I cannot endorse which I know is not my tune
but, it shall all be made crystal clear soon.
The Spirit Divine speaks to us all
if only we heed the call, heed the call!
When Father-Mother-Son summon from the inside
there in our hearts where Love likes to hide
To be our sustenance…
our food… our drink…
in the mires of evil, we shall not sink.
Satiated by Love's unconditional presence
we are purified. Our sacred essence there since
eternity,
God's own loving maternity
speaking continuously to us all
If we were to heed the Call!

Patricia

Patricia together we've wandered through the years
amidst joys and floods of tears.
Symbolically holding each other's hand
writing "I love you" in the golden sand.
The gentle lapping waves the words do not erase,
You, I and everybody this wonder does amaze.
Your steadfast spirit me does inspire
seems like sometimes you're on fire!

Apart from when the flame runs low.
Life beats out the life of the fire, so
slowly you stagger along the sandy beach
until alone that sacred space you reach.
There the words "I love you" are written in the sand
there you pause but, don't stop — this is not the
end.

A Heavenly vision comes to you from the sky
and exactly how you cannot tell, or why.
But a host of heavenly angels are seen
where dark, black, menacing clouds had been.
Their heavenly symphony fills your being
your touch, your smell, your heart, your seeing.
Your soul dances to their angelic tune
hoping it won't all suddenly end soon.
Your feet lift from above the ground,

a new peace and joy are secretly found.
Your body shining through and through
visible to me and experienced directly by you.
All worries and cares just melt away,
you ask the angels if they could stay.
They say they will as the best's yet to come,
the Son is coming and bringing His mum.
The two are longing you to salute
in great reverence and gratitude.
For when you alone in anguish and fear
in darkness and despair do shed a tear
they both are there very, very, near.

They sometimes poke you with a nudge or two
to get your attention, without hurting you.
At times they would send you a little white feather
as the clothes from on the roof you hastily gather.
These signs you sometimes ignored or missed:
"Now you must see it, we do insist!
For we have not left you to suffer alone
your feet will not be scorched or hit a stone.
On the water you shall confidently walk,
in foreign tongues to peeps you will talk
as you proclaim God's name on high,
The return of the Christ Consciousness is nigh!"

The Son and His mother appear.
The heavenly throng don't disappear

but, become even more intense
filling you, Patricia with confidence.
Your eyes lift up into the sky
and now you know exactly why!

Strewn across the sky are many a shining star
some appear right close by, others seem quite far.
The Mother humbly dressed in white and blue
holds her Son's hand as in He flew
amongst the light so dazzling bright
His body shining gold and silver white.
Both Mother and Son sweetly smile,
they've waited for this moment for a while.

Patricia is in ecstasy kneeling…
Heavenly peace, love and joy feeling…
throughout her body and into space…
gracing Patricia and the whole human race.

Thoughts suspending
Joy never-ending
Love Sublime
Peace Divine
Before smiling sadly
Now of joy and love a medley!
Not a love as humans know,
only the pure, sacred Love God can bestow.

Filling her up to the rim,
overflowing from the brim.
A taste of Heaven she has seen.
Patricia, to Heaven you have been.

Captain Plugwash

I welcome you to my den of iniquity,
established since the day of antiquity.
Let me lull you in
to my vessel of sin.
My boat violently a'rocking
with my libido shaking, shocking!

I look back at the days of old:
"You are good in bed," I had been told
and reassured, that all the right spots I knew
not needing much of a guide or a leading cue.
My fingers ran smoothly through lush terrain
valleys fruitful, overflowing with rain!

Yet, now alas the valley's run dry
and for the life of me, I don't know why?
I seem to have lost my golden touch
and perhaps try too hard — too much
effort I put into luring in
innocent women, with silk olive skin.

I cannot comprehend what has gone wrong,
how my body's stopped singing its sensual song.
My magical touch I have definitely lost
dried up valleys me now accost.
Deserts of loneliness and dry terrain

all formed due to a serious lack of rain.

I have now sadly run out of luck
and do you think I give a f**k?
Of course I do, for Heaven's sake
empty beds and bedrooms make
me seem like an old fool
who is willing to drool
over any pair of legs and bums
as my libido frustratingly hums,
wanting to entice into my 'pleasure room'
very soon, very soon, very soon!

I can't understand how they say "no".
So, I smile and my golden teeth show.
I tell them, "I am good in bed,
this to me has oft been said."
Yet, slowly and deliberately they turn away
to my utter shock and sheer dismay!

Mark

Mark, Mark, Mark, Mark, Mark,
sailing through life like the Cutty Sark.
Does he dance on his windowsill
into the small hours, until
the long-awaited sunrise
to the sun's sheer surprise?

Mark's a very kind and wonderful man
of him and his antics I am an avid fan.
His love of animals, mostly cats
but not exclusively, includes rats.
His demeanour warm and calm
to my vexed spirit a gentle balm.

He was minding his own business, when one day
I descended upon him, shall we say
as a nosey neighbour, a friendly soul
to forge a friendship, my childish goal.
I shook Mark's world to the core
as his peace and quiet were no more!

Early every morning away from me he ran
into his blessed white Transit van.
He said he was going to work, to
earn a living, but that's not true.

Since, I moved in next door
he wasn't prepared for what lay in store!

He clambers out quietly every morning,
without heeding and without warning
and into his big white van he went.
Oh, that Transit van, is heaven sent!
Every morning he drove ahead
not really going to work, instead

He would aimlessly drive across the fields
an exercise, which not much income yields.
So, he would then walk to a nondescript shop
a particular shop which would make you stop
and wonder curiously what lay behind
that old back door, what will you find?

Greeted warmly every morning it seems by
everyone
is Mark, as through the old back door is seen to
come.
What's behind that old, wooden door
all want to know — so mysterious for
Mark disappears into the ether —
no heartbeat or blood pressure meter.

Where he goes,
nobody knows.

He lands deftly on his feet
as his clients he goes to meet.
Some see him and some do not, of course.
Yet, to his gentle presence all have recourse.

He never knows on the day
which assignment's coming his way.
Will it be a saddened widow black
who needs with someone kind to chat?
Or is it a young girl bereft
all her loved ones gone, nothing's left?
Will it be an elderly man
who very sullen and lonely can
feel in his cold home and room,
hoping against hope someone'll visit soon?
Or is it a young lively lad,
beautifully turned out and smartly clad
who's been abused by a family member
and is trying to forget, not remember
drowning his sorrow in alcohol and drugs
his smart suit seeming more like rugs?
Or it is a black cat waiting to be fed,
to play and to rest on a soft, warm bed?

The list is endless, assignments vary,
yet Mark's always cheerful, not wary.
He takes it all in his stride
A mind open and heart wide
full of compassion, gentle and kind

whatever's the assignment, he doesn't mind.
He always smiles first
to satiate their thirst
for a friendly face
full of Love's grace.

To those who him they cannot see,
invisible to them sadly he has to be!
Yet, his wings flutter warmly around their being
albeit, they can't see him with their own eyes
seeing.
His wings of white, silver and glittering gold,
he wraps around them and in love enfold.
They feel a sudden calm descend
as love's peace and joy he does send.
He gives them from the dark, some respite
filling their world with some needed light.

To those who see him as of the flesh
as his angelic being a body does enmesh,
He speaks calmly and softly of things
which make his invisible wings
flutter and of joy and peace sing.
These beings look on and behold
in truth what they are being told.
A gentle man taking the time
to bring light to their darkness, making all shine.
His words and gentle presence making it all fine.

79

When he leaves to go back home in his white Transit van,
his wings fold back neatly in as he turns back into a man.
He smiles at the success of each assignment completed
heading home sometimes, somehow depleted.
He hopes his neighbour is tucked safely inside
so that from her nosiness, he doesn't have to hide!
As shattered after a day's good work he can be
this for all is very plain to see.
Except for his nosey neighbour Mary,
who is and has been always quite contrary.
She pounces on him as he drives back
not cutting him any slack
for the long day he'd pretended to be grafting in wood
His angelic assignments fulfilling, as he faithfully could.
Not many this side of Mark knew,
his neighbour Mary, one amongst the few!

VOLUME II — THE PLAYING FIELDS

"Where shall we all gather
as we come to play together
Shall we make it the swings?"
Voice after voice rings.

Light Versus Dark

I touched Evil this weekend
in its rawest, most visible sense.
Evil's face anger, ego and fear
with Peace and Love dispense.

I saw the Face of Evil
contorting looking 'graceful'
a pretence to fool and beguile,
isn't this so disgraceful?

What is described as evil
is what it's always been
able to influence thought forms,
contort what is plainly seen.

The power of evil to deceive
the pure of heart contort,
Reality it has the secret power
to insidiously distort.

Evil operates in the dark,
it works covertly, underhand.
Open your eyes and ears to see it
and you will understand.

Once you comprehend its game

and get the hang of all its rules,
You can use your own Light power
and not be taken in, as fools.

The Light power, it too is potent
we forget how silently strong
it operates to dispel darkness,
exposing all that is wrong!

You have the power to manifest
you have the power to heal
you know who you are and who I AM,
My love in you I seal.

You have the power to see
You possess the gift to know
Embrace the grace of Divine Love
which on you abundant blessings does bestow.

If the light is not hidden,
If on tall lamp-posts exposed,
then Darkness gets a shock
for its darkness is disposed.

The darker the darkness,
the greater the Light.
The deeper the evil
the brighter the Light shines bright.

The greater the evil,
the greater the Grace.
Allow your light to shine,
its luminance embrace.

Hidden in the depths of each heart
forever there it's been,
Allow it to shine out through
the brightest you've ever seen.

Evil hates the light shining bright
It makes it turn away
and like an evil wounded Beast
writhing in pain, begins to sway.

"Connect to the light within
allow it bright to shine.
Believe in your Divinity.
My Light is also Thine."
(Sacred Cosmic Consciousness)

Morning, night and afternoon

Is Davide Icke the David?
Shall I meet him soon?
When and if I do,
shall it be morning or afternoon?

I would like to read my poems
to the whole world very soon.
Is my time slowly approaching,
will it be morning or afternoon?

I need to minister to humanity.
Is it going to be soon?
Shall I be healing humanity
in the morning or afternoon?

This weekend I touched Evil.
Will it be ending soon?
Its far-reaching destruction
comes every morning and afternoon.

At night time it flourishes.
Will that be changing soon?
The urge to coerce, control, destroy,
will it end morning, night or afternoon?

Will the whole of humanity be restored

and will it be very soon?
Will they be playing freely in the school
playground again, every morning and afternoon?

Will our children jump and skip
and will they be hugging soon?
Hands-to-hands clapping to tunes
some mornings and afternoons.

Will our children hear the song
of birds tweeting and singing soon?
Will they know Nature before it dies
one morning, night or afternoon?

5G poisons rivers and all of Earthly life,
will people recognise this soon?
Birds dropping dead, fishes dread
the water, every morning, night and afternoon.

Will our children ever breathe fresh air?
Or shall they all die soon?
Wearing   masks,   divisive   tasks,   controlling
conditioning
every morning, night and afternoon.

By the River I sat

It's still, peaceful by the riverbank
the sun dances before my eyes
the waters gently shine, shimmer:
leaves dancing softly
birds chirping happily
boats silently waddling along
bedazzling reflections on the water
gentle waves waltz and jive.
Silver lights on green leaves glisten
trees, water, grass all silently listen
to the perfect symphony of Creation
as originally the sacred Life, Love, Light did
fashion.

Boats make the still water ripple
like it's drunk too many a tipple!
Instantaneously, the water regains calm
to my vexed spirit a soothing balm.
Birds singing their melodious song
their tune added to the heavenly throng.
On branches as they sit and sing
with open hearts their songs they bring
a chorus of heavenly angels choir
which one cannot help but admire.
A yellow leaf suddenly falls
My name "Mary" it softly calls.

I smile and enjoy our little game
with the innocence of a child, no shame.
I remember we are told to be born once more
so that our loving God we can humbly adore.
It's to be dazzled by the Father's creation
Mother's benevolence for every creed and every
nation.

The light and shadows continue to play
their own hidden message to us they relay.
In this setting of light and dark
the light in contrast to dark, is stark.
One cannot at this moment see the light
if it weren't dark, ever so slight.
Yet, the light that within us lies latent
sometimes hidden in the heart, mistaken
for the dark
the light's forgotten
covered in shadow
no shape or form
no outward bodily norm.
Just like the sun hidden by a cloud
inside it'll stay till out it's allowed
hidden behind a veil, covered by a shroud.

But, when the dark shadowy shroud is shifted
the dark veil covering the light, is lifted.
Iridescent lights shimmer and glimmer galore
exposing beauty, joy, love full of Heaven's lore!

The soul ecstatically dances
as the light it all enhances.
A beauteous bounty it makes unfold
like that seldom seen and rarely told.

Whispers of the Oak

I walked along the fields briskly
on a sunny autumnal day.
The oak tree whispered in my ear
this is what it had to say:

"Come child, come child, closer, closer
I love it when you walk past me
you look in awe and wonder
seeing not just a majestic tree.

You look up ahead at my acorns
as they hang so daintily
like little crystal chandeliers,
is this what you can see?

My trunk ever so ancient
it looks so big and strong,
The Wisdom that it's created
to you and all does belong.

I have gathered my Wisdom wisely,
years of standing in my field
observing all that's around me
does silence, Wisdom yield.

I watch quietly the comings
and the goings of the birds
singing like a heav'nly choir
their song surpassing words.

I listen to the lapping water
the sound puts me to sleep.
Lap, lap, lap a' lapping
all the way to the creek.

The gentle breeze's sweet soft strokes
I relish and hold very dear.
For when her gentle blows caress me
all my worries disappear.

The autumn's wind wild whispers
become very loud
when winter approaches
with a crash-banging sound.

I stand tall as its cacophony
deafening billowing breath
blows fiercely through me
sounding like Death.

I watch Death simply
as my leaves Fall.
It doesn't grieve me
no, not at all!

For I do not believe,
yet for sure I do know
Death into Life dances
as spring opens its door.

New leaves spring forth
Oh, how I rejoice
as I come back to life
a brand-new look entice.

The Earth keeps me safe
feet deeply and firmly planted
or trunk shall I say,
will surely not be supplanted.

I wait for your passing
in quiet expectation
my roots listen out
without hesitation."

At Warborough Green

Dear Yeshua, Jesus God's Son
Your long-lost mother's now come
to be your mother once more
got her foot through the back door.
Her heart's overflowing with love for You
for all that You are and all that You do!

Inside my womb I carried You silently
You were formed in there almost unwittingly.
I loved having You deep inside my womb
The living Son of God in a live loving tomb.
Your true nature and all ours wholly Divine
our bodies a temple, its host all thine,
as You grow slowly and delicately form
I nurtured your being I, Your mom!

It felt like I'd always known You from evermore
when the angel appeared though, I wasn't so sure!
Then little by little as You slowly 'n' silently
formed inside me
the truth of who You are and who I am I could
clearly see.
I felt so much love as inside me You grew
not only love, but a deep peace too!

On the day You deemed to come out,

around midday or thereabout
I laughed with every contraction
for labour at its inception
was not hard labour or a hard chore.
Heavenly assisted was Your birth for
as we know from millennia before
You are the Son of God incarnated
showing us how evil can be disseminated.
You are the Son showing us how, the Way
to Your Heavenly Father-Mother without delay.
It is now pertinent that all heed Your call, please
make us fit
to regain our child-like purity as from before the
split.

Musings for the Month of May
(from the Blessed Virgin Mary)

You are the Ultimate space holder,
Chaos, disharmony are not of you
yet You hold them within with so much love
Joy, peace, compassion and playfulness too.

I'm so grateful for the month of May
the most beautiful one I would say
to have it dedicated to me
is a great honour, this I can see.

Flowers blossoming in full bloom
flourishing fresh fruits coming soon.
Bright clear skies and the sun above
all beaming Light Life-giving Love.

For the honour of what I am called to do
for me, You and all of humanity too,
I am grateful beyond words can express
my joy and thankfulness, I cannot repress.

I have got responsibilities too
No one to be lost, um… or just a few.
Those who persist to shut their heart
pride and ego, playing a major part.

The rest shall all come running to You
back in their Heart, Your Love imbue.
There they'll stay forever more
as they come rushing, by the score!

Let's receive them every one
come in, rest and have some fun,
by special invite from Father-Mother-Son
we all celebrate, for we are all One.

The Wedding

I watch from a distance the Wedding today
as I can't be present in any other way.
It would've been lovely to have been there
but I am here, I can't be everywhere!

This celebration of Love touches the heart
as the couple promise from Love never to part.
They promise to reflect on Earth, God's love
and to be as pure and sacred on Earth, as is above.

Healing each other through life's ups and downs
Smiling gently through life's little frowns.
Not taking themselves ever too seriously
relishing in each other, the other's mystery.

Allowing each other the space
to be themselves and not erase
that which, who they are, unique
not eliminating that wondrous streak.

Humility is the key.
There isn't just 'me'
we celebrate our unity
with our Life, Love, Light Trinity.

A blank canvas new

God's paintbrush light hue
The couple paint
a picture quaint.

They are able to reflect
God's love, not neglect.
Reminding humanity of values lost
bringing them back: "Oh how beautiful!"

Flimkien magħqudin
m'aħniex imxerdin —
Ġesu' f'nofsna dejjem ikun
b'imħabba qawwija bħal tal-Ljun!

Kemm iħobbna Ġesu' tagħna
Hu qiegħed dejjem magħna.
F'daż-żwieg magħqudin
f'Alla u b'imħabbtu meħlusin.

Sliema u Qaddisa ngħidu llum
ħalli din l-Imħabba tkun
mqawwija bil-Qawwa t'Alla u t'Ommu
b'tifħir qawwi dejjem f'fommu (u fommħa).

Two are now One.
One their total sum.
Each unique, by far
a bright shining star.

An inspiring painting
patiently waiting
to be made completed,
with colour resplendent.

Through thick and thin
without and within
May Love grace this unity
in Time and Eternity.

WEAREONE

My Love's here to sustain
in you It'll always remain.
Do not fret or be afraid
The Son-Daughter of God you are made.
Enjoy the rest of your Earthly sojourn
until I return, until I return!

The Angel of doubt is near
Do not lend him your ear.
He comes to confuddle and confuse
your attention him, you must refuse.
Shut your eyes and turn away
Lest your Will, he does sway.

Jealous of your new connection strong
Nothing now can really go wrong!
Things might appear strange and weird
don't be afraid — nothing's to be feared!
For as I promise, so shall I perform
My Word is My Truth, this is my norm.

My Word is true, it holds forever more
you've now come in and opened the door
to My Kingdom in Heaven here on Earth,
experienced Its glory and all Its worth.
With one foot in through the door,

you needn't be scared or worried any more!

'Mistakes' are mistakes no more
as I, pure Love looked and saw
your heart so full overflowing, so
any 'mistakes' that you do make
I change to blessings, for your sake!

It's beautiful how sacred Love all transforms
into beauty, joy, peace creating new forms
and ways of being, procured
new ways of seeing secured.
A new Heaven inside you sings
its bell within your being rings
and reverberates throughout
face, eyes, ears and mouth
proclaiming My Love
vibrating below and above
dissipating all your shame
as you are enveloped in my Love, in my Holy
Name.

VOLUME III — THE END GAME

"How long are you able to stay out?"
I hear all my playmates shout.
"Up until it's dinnertime," I say
as my mum's sweet call I must obey.

Used and Abused

We are all being used and abused by the Cabal, Elite and their systems, platforms, corporations, etcetera. This poem can be taken symbolically and or literally, individually or addressing the whole of the human race. It speaks to each and every one of us. Take from it what you need. It is when you recognise and acknowledge abuse in any shape or form, that you can make the decision either to go along with it or to put an end to it. The options may seem endless. The choice is one.

Poet
The world is currently upside down
Trying to smile, instead I frown!
Tears strolling down my cheeks
my whole body shakes and my spirit weeps.
Why is this happening to us, why?
I can hardly breathe, just about sigh.
Why, oh why won't we open our eyes
Call a spade a spade, and untruths lies?
Why are our hearts so closed to care?
Why are we not loving, don't we dare?
Stinging darts
Broken hearts
Shattered dreams

Battered screams
Silent anguish
Beaten language
Sighing breaths
Brutal deaths.

The Godhead — Manifest Divine Father, Mother, Son; sacred Life, Love, Light, reverberating within the sound of Unmanifest Divine, Sacred, infinite Cosmic Consciousness. Nevertheless, an EXPERIENCE beyond any name, label, word, description, concept, person.

"When my children come back to me,
my passionate love for them they will see.
Return to My Heart of Love and know,
All My Love on YOU, I yearn to bestow.
Your bodies abused
Your embodiment used"

Poet
for someone else's wild wiles
whose depravity beguiles
Freedom silently stifles.

The Abusers — The Cabal, The Elite — deep state; deep church and anybody who has abused their power and people's trust — abuse can be mental, physical, sexual, psychological, emotional, or all of the above. It not only happens on an individual level, but on a global level as is now and has been throughout the history of humankind!

They prey on innocent children's blood
their narcissistic ego they fully flood
with the need to coerce, control and destroy
by means they can overtly and covertly employ.
Their weakness exhibited
their love non-existent
their private parts minute,
their whole being destitute!

Their insides rotting, vile.
Their lungs all the while
exhaling poisoned air
but, do they care?
The evils within them smile,
appearing 'sweet' all the while!
A heart made of stone
room for self-love alone.
Their eyes dart out hate
poisoned words, like bait.
The children young get stung
laid out there naked, hung
on a line of deception
for at its inception
EVIL

LIES
its foundation
deceit, to defile
an innocent child (or adult, or nation or the whole
wide world — all of humanity!).

Justice is coming, it's on its way.
They'll all be made accountable come what may.
The last judgement is near
You need not shed a tear.
Yet, they shall face it in fear!

The Abused

Individuals, children, teenagers and adults as well
as all of us who have been tricked by Evil's scare-
mongering schemes, underhand tactics to coerce,
control and destroy us ALL. The abuser thrives on
secrecy, secret societies, secret agendas and will
torture and kill those who whistle-blow or go
against the flow. Those who do, are the martyrs of
our time!

Their return long-awaited
Anger, fear now abated
As closer to themselves they draw
seeing this is not their fault or flaw,
but the debasement of their abuser
vile, defunct, f**king child user.

The child knows they are pure within
that their whole being's free from sin.
They recognise that this is abuse
to face it squarely, they don't refuse.
They tell themselves once and for all
"I must tell, it's my shout, my call.
I will explode if I keep it all in
It needs to come out what lies within
I need to verbally and openly express
my sense of shame and worthlessness.
I wish someone would listen without any
judgement,
see the coercion, manipulation — it's not called
abuse
for nothing! It was always so damned hard to
refuse.
Seemed at times there was no way to say "No,"
I carried the shame and the guilt so
Nobody would know!

That mental torture and bodily shame
I feel like a person without a name!
Obliterated is the sense of who I am, you see,
I feel as debased, defiled and dirty as can be.
I shower for hours, but the dirt seems to stick
I've had to protect myself with a wall made of
brick.

I was always told if I were to tell,

the bell of death, its knell
would ring inside my parents' ears
a swamp of blood and a pool of tears
will overthrow my mother in despair
a state so shocking beyond repair.
My father would believe me not
as emotional intelligence he has not got.
He would disown me as defiled
He would say that I have lied.
A way out there was not one
it's OK for you and some
others, who have not been abused
for others' amusement have not been used.
It's not so bad for such a one
You've got freedom, I have none!

This shell I inhabit in darkness and fear
I don't like others getting too near
Lest they smell anguish and touch my pain
I must not let them that vantage point gain.

I'd like to believe in my everyday life I'm in
complete control,
for when my abusers the deadly dice doth roll
I have to dance to their tune and perform on their
cue
The rest of time, control is MY due!

I think I control what I do, how and when

outside the iniquity of their soulless den.
I put most of that abuse aside
Deep in my psyche, I let it hide.

I hope that buried there deep within
away from full view, it rests therein.
I am on constant guard lest it comes out
and in full throttle it will begin to shout:

The Inner voice of Truth ushering forth from the
depths, within where it's been buried deeply
hidden. Now ready to be exposed and freed from
the tyranny of secrecy and silence.

"Of my innocence you have robbed me
slain my self, till all I can see
is a shadow of the being I am meant to be.
Like a thief you have left me bare
I cannot go anywhere
where this shadow doesn't go
where f**king shame doesn't show
where control consumes, fears abide
a state of being, where I cannot hide!
My being — my being no more
you come like a thief and force the back door.
Your scheming ways full of lies and deceit
are a crossroads where Evil, a Psychopath meet.
You offer me money, toys and expensive treats
You buy me delicious meals and unusual sweets.

I don't care for these artificial goods and things
I'd rather have my being back and a strong set of
wings
to fly away every time you come near me
saying money is power as you enter me, you see!

You say I enjoy it as much as you do
and if I say no, you say…"

The Abuser The manipulation of the abuser
sometimes subtle, at others much more overt. Its
ultimate aim to feed its need to coerce, control and
destroy. The intention is always self-serving
feeding greed and lust.

"you'll know I'll tell who!
Your mother or father or preferably both.
Would you like to encounter your own father's
wrath?
Or would you like to face your mother's disbelief
as you openly disclose and sigh a sigh of relief?
She will not take your side. She won't believe you
I'm her family and she loves me too
as much as a son, if not even more.
Don't dare to speak up and settle the score!
Don't you dare tell our secret little child
if you know what's good for you, Hide!
I'll deny it all till I'm blue in the face,
you'll be called a liar and just in case

you are not scared enough of speaking out,
I am the adult and I can shout
louder than you, I have more clout
you'll fail miserably if you decide to come out!
But if you keep our little snide secret safe and
sound
pressies, holidays and all shall abundantly abound.
You should never materially lack
although your soul I have smeared black.
I have tainted all of your being
open your eyes, I own your own seeing!
I dictate when we do it, how and where,
I decide what toys we use
as I now use and abuse
your body, mind, heart and soul for my
own amusement!
You may ask, why? Oh, why?

I'll simply say it's because I can
You are the boy — I am the man.
I call the shots and you bow down
You are the slave — I wear the crown.
I will get away with this, you know
nobody will get to know, friend or foe.
I control every aspect of this situation
I end the session as I procure initiation.
I am almighty, powerful and strong
you are little, powerless and always wrong.
I, of sound mind and of body too

all that I say and do is always true.
You are worthless, but not when I call
not when I ram you from the back on the wall.
You are so worthless, but not when we shag
not whilst I thrust it all in a bag.
I am not insane, or mentally deranged
it is the world that is changed, oh so changed!
I am not evil, sinister or bad
only a demon — YOU'VE BEEN HAD!
I am not going to go to hell and slowly burn
as my abuse makes your stomach churn.
You are the one who'll carry Guilt and Shame
I'll go scot-free with a clear name.
No shame shall ever stick with me
as I cover my tracks, ever so carefully.
You are the one who will be shamed, if you go
public you will be blamed.
They will think what a terrible thing he has done,
I hope that he's punished, that little piece of scum."

Poet

As you can see
you, me and everybody
the abuser lies through his rotten teeth
manipulates, coerces, scares and terrifies
his behaviour with awful threats dignifies.
Fear is his currency,
Threats his warranty.
The abuse is not just sexual,

114

but physical, emotional and mental.
They gas light their shame
as Humanity takes all the blame
stripping us all of our sovereign name!

But, not forever more!
For one day very soon, they'll all have to settle the score.
All the defilement that they did to ONE AND ALL
is what they will suffer themselves and much, much more.
Whether here on Earth, or in a hellish hell
I am sorry to say which, I cannot really tell.
But, as they did do to others, so to them it shall be done.
They have defiled God's Daughters — abused God's Sons.
The Law of the Universe won't let them off scot-free
Justice must reign, for Peace to be.
For their sins, past, present, and future
they must make up
As their incestuous guilt and shame
will not shut up!

Innocence Lost

Friend, fiend or foe?
This is what I really want to know.
Did he fiddle with my son's innocence
under the guise of love, such pretence?
Did his filthy, f**king hands touch my
Son's delicate parts if so, I ask why
was it to satiate his lustful desire?
I hope his soul burns in eternal fire!
Did he deliberately undress my son
from his innocence, for his own fun?
His own self-gratification satiated,
my son's own embodiment repudiated.
His menacing touch molesting
my son's intimacy, his being infesting
with anger and fear which are not of him
filling him with his own evil satanic din.
My son's being like a silken robe ripped,
of his innocence and purity brutally stripped.
Being made to feel dirty
dodging his abuser's flirty
looks, which the son try to seduce
his being with chaos and confusion infuse.
How can that adult sleep at night,
he must know what he does, isn't right?
When he lays his head on his comfy bed,
why can't it be on a bed of nails instead

When he dreams of blue oceans far and wide,
why can't he see prison cells, in which to hide
and into them ride on a great black stallion
wearing of Satan a big black medallion?
And once trapped inside those four thick walls
all his own clothing to the floor suddenly falls.
He looks at himself stark naked, in the nude,
whilst others snigger and sneer. "Isn't that rude?"
I think not, for from behind this bar
I'm glad to say, he can't go very far.
All the other inmates want "a piece of him"
Oh, sweet, sweet revenge much sweeter than sin:
Avenging what he had done,
to her pure, innocent young son!

They look wide-eyed at his pathetic private part,
pointing at it mocking: "Huh, it's no work of art!"
This thin, small rubber-like pipe, like a tiny seed
controlling his lustful appetite and fuelling greed
would not yield fruit juicy and deliciously messy,
yields only, rotten dried up crops, nothing fleshy.
His delirious desires of the flesh arise,
from Satan's subtle temptations, I surmise!
For the flesh is pure until
demons are invited in. Still
abiding in that greed and lust
flamed stronger by gust after gust
of wind that bellows the fire,
of lustful, sinful, wild desire.

The prison bars are very strong,
showing him what he'd done wrong!
His inmates violent to the core,
the upper hand he has no more!
There is now no innocent child
with whom to go sexually wild.
There are only inmates gagging,
their tantalising tongues wagging
as this newbie stark naked stands
whilst Satan with his hot iron brands
His name on his servant's body exposed
into a living hell he is being deposed.

The piping red hot brand instils
and his violent, vile being fills
with anger, jealousy, lust and greed
which now full-grown, no longer seed
are the fuel that spurn his action
within this evil, demonic, satanic faction.
Inside the prison cell he'll stay,
eating meals of straw and hay.
Behind the bars he does despair,
his being going into disrepair.

One by one, his limbs give way
dissolving into hellish fires, shall we say?!
His mind, it stays intact and sees
the body's misery as it wees
onto the prison cell cold floor

just behind the locked prison door.
The stench fills the thick four walls
as urine's condensed droplet after droplet falls
like a sickly yellow vomit-like rain, sticky
all the other inmates, taking the mickey!
How did he fall into such a state,
and of this prison become an inmate?
He catches a glimpse of his face, its reflection clear,
denotes his evil-doing. I'm so sorry my Dear
Son, for at his hands you alone had to suffer,
with no release, comfort or friendly buffer
to ease your anguish and release your pain,
injected with fear, guilt and endless shame
as he played with your being his satanic game.

You, just an innocent child
loving life and going wild
as the Earth's beauteous song
rings in your ears all day long.

You, innocently playing with toys,
a little boy who playing enjoys,
indoors and outdoors too
at times alone, at others me and you.

My heart you filled with beauty and light,
our love one for the other shone ever so bright.
Yet, the symphony got rudely interrupted

as your being got violently abducted
by this evil force inside this demonic man's heart,
to destroy you completely, his plot's crucial part.

For he corrupted your innocence
stole your sovereign freedom
controlled your little boyish body
thwarted your creative, moulding mind
stained the purity of your pure God-given soul
for his own evil, lustful goal!

I go back to the prison walls,
where the cold floor suddenly falls
and gives way like in a quake
in which all prison cells shake.
Suddenly, a hole like a portal opens up,
a vortex wide open which cannot shut.

His heart sinks
his breath stinks
As Death breathes
and life leaves
his body bereft.
A legal theft.

Taking him
to the place of Sin.
He looks on, dejected
his being with fear injected,

as his feet lose their grip
on the crumbling floor slip
Deeper into the vortex he's sucked in.
Has he yet reached the place of Sin?
His body spins
speed wins
the battle of time
as he pays for his abominable crime.

Swiftly and suddenly his feet give way
his beaten body and mind begin to sway.
He seems to be quickly gathering speed
groans, shrieks of anguish his ears heed.
Closer into sin he now falls.
Suddenly he stops. His body crawls
through a long, dark deep tunnel
slowly through it he needs to funnel
and fumble through to the other side,
where hellish groans and shrieks abide.

He wishes he could get stuck,
but he's now running out of luck!
For you see on the Earthly plane,
on others he inflicted pain.
Now the tables have been somehow turned,
all his control, coercion and fun adjourned.
He longed to go back to ask forgiveness
but, stuck in the funnel he is
dying to do a stinking piss

and a sickening, stench-filled fart
which he'd perfected, as a work of art!
For the demons within had cursed his body to die
and in this evil stinking cesspit lie.
But he is left empty bereft of all
NOTHING is there, NOTHING at all!

He suddenly wishes he were dead,
that would've stopped this hell, and instead
of anguish, agony and a loss of control, he'd be
singing with the angels, ever so happily!

What, oh what had gone so suddenly wrong?
Why is he robbed of singing his song?
How has it all come to a sudden end,
and where do these demons his soul send?
He had been a loyal and faithful trooper
always obedient to Satan's edicts, super!
Now is he punished for a loyal, faithful servant to
have been
always following the precepts of Satan's evil
scheme
Coercing, controlling, destroying all that is good
as a dark angel of Satan faithfully should.
Mocking and demeaning all that is innocent and
pure
smearing it with the black blood of Belzebub, for
sure.
He demands to know where is his reward,

as out of the funnel, he heads down toward
what seems like a bottomless pit
full of urine, vomit and stinking s**t.

The answer echoes, but the message gets thwart'd,
as the crashing speed the sound vibrations contorted.
"You have had your reward already, mate,
as your greed and lust I did fully satiate
to the brim and overflowing
subtly veiling your inner knowing
mostly through your ego impure
making you think you are pure. Huh, for sure!
Your guilt did not let you quietly lie
as the innocence of children you beguile
and seek to corrupt to the core,
bringing them crashing violently to the floor.
Feeding off crumbs from your sumptuous meal
stomach churning, heart emptied finding it hard to feel
any love, warmth or affection
at your satanic, evil infection.
Just emptiness, the worst state of being procured,
your faithful service, your soul has secured.
Of course, it cannot now be spared,
as in this funnel, in this tunnel nothing can be repaired.
What you'd done, you'd knowingly and willingly done,

in the meantime, having oodles and oodles of fun!
You were warned early on what working for me means,
your childhood teachings did many years ago spill the beans!
So, an excuse like 'I didn't know!'
will not set you free to go!
Oh no! Oh no! Oh no!

If you think that this is bad,
then sorry mate, I'm very sad
to say, there's much worse coming your way
as in this hell you've chosen to come and stay.
You had been given chance after chance
to change the tune and the moves to your dance.
But sadly for you, but not for me
You chose on my path to continually be.
My road like a highway wide,
most are tricked into driving this side
being taken in by glitz and speed
my lustful ways they faithfully heed.
My noise muffles their inner knowing
in them jealousy, lust and greed growing.
Nothing was never ever enough
of the material and sexual stuff.

With me, you worked hard to destroy what Love creates
poisoning the seeds Love sows, as It patiently

waits
for them to fruition come
pouncing on innocent daughter and son.
I riled you in with empty promises sweet
I do many others too, whom this same fate shall
meet.
The most dreaded state of being in my realm you
shall embrace,
the state of being nothing — Nothingness as you
fall from God's Grace.
To be in a state with nowhere to hide,
your Nothingness to know and in it forever abide
Is the worst state of being you shall ever know
as your sins stand before you and your mind it
doth show.
You are rightly terrified at what lays in store
being denied the glories of Heavenly lore.
You are scared of being Nothing, so
you shriek with fear and terror know.
What you dished out to boys and girls
comes to haunt you now. It all unfurls
before your eyes, as you see your sin
throwing the life of others into the bin.
As you fall deeper into the pit
clambering through stinking s**t
you wish you had chosen a different path
to avoid this hellish aftermath.
Yet, many would agree and rightly so,
that this state of hell you must know.

As you made others suffer at your hands
concocting evil, shameful plans
forgetting that one day
in a state of hell you shall stay
from which there is no respite
no wings for you to take flight
and touch the Life, Love, Light, so
Sacred Love you shall not know.
Your evil before your eyes shall forever beam
into an infernal eternity, it may seem."

A Human Heart

Here I sit with nothing to give you
Here I am with nothing to do!
My new heart's like a road map
each crack
representing a road I've gone down
sinking, swimming or about to drown.
Lurking in the water's essence
of good and evil there is presence.
A road map to show the terrain
weeded, manured overflowing with grain.

It has been battered this heart of mine
but, through the mercy of Love Divine
it has been mended and made into One
from all the shattered pieces it's been done!
All the paths within it show
the Grace of Love thereupon it bestow'd
and bound together like with glue,
the minute pieces and big ones too.
All bound back together into a tapestry
of which each part is a mystery.

I look at my new heart to me given
I know my wrongdoings are all forgiven.
I see that my essential being's pure
It radiates light and love, for sure.

There is nothing else for me to do
just sit like a cow in a field and "moo".
No judgment, no blame or shame
no winning or losing, this is not a game!
Just being in the present moment
with no commentary or vile comment.
Accountable only to my Creator,
basking in the pure Love of my Maker.

The world has taught me to detest
who I am and all the rest.
To be like this, and say like that
to be thin and not be fat
to have dyed hair
and lots of flair.
To always act as if I don't care!
To value what on the outside lies
to not value life, as time flies.
To give up my life to the State
not count the cost, at any rate!

This all serves the deep church and state
Wake up we must, before it's too late!
Our life-force they feed off for their own empire
our blood sucked out, for like a vampire
they stick their jagged teeth into our neck
transforming Humanity into a nervous wreck.

I reject their shameless laws
all their mandates full of flaws.
I cannot by their regs abide
Neither can I my true truth hide.
When in the end all's said and done
I pray, "Love may your Kingdom come."
May it be here as it is there,
may we reflect Your Love and Light everywhere!

Love's own protect and put aside
In Love's pure essence abide.
Do not let them go asunder
with evil blunder after blunder.

This sorry state of affairs
since the split it occurs.
It has been the root of all evil,
the inception of the devil.

This poem is not just for me
as I watch a broken humanity.
It's all unfolding before my eyes
all the untruths, all the lies!

I'm not sure what I'm meant to do
as I sit with no agenda, am I meant to?
Not looking behind at the past,
at this lifetime, it won't last.
I sit and wait and watch and wait

will this my fear and anguish abate?
I sit with no expectation
no intended outcome
no agenda
no loss
no gain.
I just sit
with
what is.
You are my ALL
in You I sit tall,
as all is ONE
I sit in You and in everyone!

My body silently throbs
with an anguish that life robs.
My soul silently weeps
with a sadness that deeply seeps
into my veins, my every pore
into my gut right down into my core.
My heart cries a tear of blood red.
"Why?" my broken heart sadly said.

There doesn't seem to be an end to my pain,
is this part of my motherly reign?
The honour is mine, the pain is too,
you do feel it like I do?
Do you experience this being of joy bereft,
leaving me stark naked with nothing left?

It isn't how it should be, I know
there should now be joy wherever I go
but this is how it is at the minute
I shall stay with it and go within it.
Without struggling to let it go,
just staying with it, let it be so!
And when it's done its job, played its part
I acknowledge and thank it, it may depart.
It would've left an indelible mark
on the map of my sensitive heart.
Each mark a lesson has me to teach
until the end of that mark I reach.
The map's unending roads and lanes
lead me to places with no names.
As I arrive, there I sit still
I do not move, not until
each and every sensation within me I feel
whether I sit, stand or kneel.
It's so hard just being still
with nothing to do, not until
the sensations move
with nothing to prove
to fix or improve.
Breath bellows forth
from south or from north
filling my lungs with life
cold, cutting like a sharp knife.
If only I could somewhere hide
where Fear and Anguish subside.

If only I could go inside
and there rest in perfection true
where I am not judged by me or by you.

This self-judgement like a blood-thirsty bat arrives
my inner life juices for itself derives.
It makes for itself its own juice,
its own life-force wanting to spruce.
It leaves me feeling quite depleted,
not quite so self-completed.
Do I need to batter myself like this?
Wouldn't it better I gave myself a hug 'n' a kiss?
Wouldn't my being relish some compassion
to grow in love, joy and in life passion?

Wouldn't my being want some fun?
Wouldn't it want to be One with everyone?
Does it want to be battered and beaten
Like a delicacy, savagely eaten?

No, it does NOT, for self-respect I have got.
I know my own worth as from my birth!
I know deep down I am worthy of love and respect
for the whole of my being, its every aspect.
If only I know this deep down at the core
where fear and fear of fear are no more.
If only I know this at soul-level so deep
then all self-abasement shall not make me weep.

If only I know this in every pore of my being
and see it always with my inner eye's seeing.
Then nothing and nobody shall hold the key
to my birth right sovereignty and life-long liberty.

The Playground

They symbol of the Rainbow
so drastically has changed
and by this evil ruling Cult
its meaning rearranged!

It used to simply symbolise
the covenant between Love and Man.
Nothing will ever come between them
Do you think it can?

Not even our own evil,
not any less our sin
can ever keep away Love's love
from coming forth and being within.

For Inside — our very Essence
is the Infinite spark of Love Divine
who in Its image us created
"I've made you, you are mine!

Not to coerce, control or worse destroy
but, to enjoy your brief Earthly sojourn
in these playing fields to freely roam
as to enjoy and cherish it you learn.

For joy is the highest of vibrations

it lifts up all those who
come to the playing fields to play,
everyone's invited and YOU are too!"

The swings a wind of joy create
their motion to and fro
everybody can freely enjoy
you needn't be a pro!

The thrill of the slide as you sit at the top,
just before you simply let yourself go
whooshing down at neck-breaking speed
Life's worries away quickly billow and blow.

The merry-go-round reminds us all
that "what goes around comes around,"
making all so deliriously dizzy and
not everybody's cup of tea, I found.

The tall trees in the playground
protect both the old and young
As they unite in having fun
their songs not left unsung.

The shrieks of joyous laughter
ring in the playground's air,
filling it with love and joy
spreading swiftly everywhere.

It's sad to see a playground empty
no children allowed in.
The gravest of our century's travesty
the gravest, greatest mortal sin.

Replacing the children's fun and laughter
is that dreaded poster of a rainbow in colour.
Substituting fun and life in the playground
Death fills it like no other.

So, sadly now the rainbow symbol rife and
everywhere
as you go in and out of shops and everywhere you
stare,
A symbol of Death and Darkness it has suddenly
become
as the Cabal, Cult, the one percent control the
whole world as one.

The colours shining bright on paper, are still,
lifeless and dead
as children now going to the playground, are
being made to dread.
We adults, protectors of our children have a lot to
do.
We must set our children free, without much
further ado.

In so doing, saving our children from this tyranny
we shall be saving ourselves too, I'm sure this you
can see!

So, get off that sofa and "subito"*, smash that
beastly black box,
summon all your strength, courage and the
cleverness of a fox.
Empower your free will, call on your creativity,
open your mind too
bring the children back to the empty playground
and bring yourself — yes, YOU!

Do NOT comply, do NOT consent, do NOT
acquiesce — **SAY NO!**
Don't give your freedom and breath away to an
Evil Elite who YOU gravely mistreat!
They've taken the symbolism of the Rainbow and
replaced it with black Death,
taken our Children, our Freedom, our Livelihoods
— and lastly, our Life — our Breath.

An end to this we must procure
and we must do it soon.
For their evil plan as it unfolds,
is the whole playground to ruin.

We must act fast, we must act NOW
tomorrow might be too late

as they barricade the playground
and lock up its front and back gate.
"Do NOT comply, do NOT consent — unite
together as ONE —
THIS IS THE ONLY WAY — we once again can
have some fun!
THIS IS THE ONLY WAY — this war's going to
be WON!
THIS IS THE ONLY WAY — our new life now will
have begun!"

* Subito is Italian for, 'immediately', 'right away', 'at once'

The End Game

I had a dream
What does it mean?
For the life of me
I cannot see!

<u>Dominic</u>

A solemn, secretive young lady in black
surrounded by black front and back.
A long black coat to the floor she wore
I'm sure that's not all that I saw.

Her long, straight black hair
was pitch-black dark, not fair.
It almost swept the dark black floor
matching the black coat she wore.

I could only see her back
as she stood there clad in black
slim, sullen and tall.
I suddenly hear her call:

"Get the scissors as I stand
for this hair please understand,
needs to be cut short
most of it, I must abort.

And this long fur-edged black coat,
hanging on me like a black goat
drags me down with its weight
it shortly needs to meet its Fate.

Come, quick this coat do cut
short, shorter — and that door pleeease do SHUT!
Lest a draft comes into this room
or a ray of light, as it's morning soon."

The servants hurried to the door
they suddenly appeared by the score
to execute her raucous orders
they flew in, from across the borders.

And from across the miles
all straight-faced, serious — no smiles.
A harsh demeanour all exhibited
a cold reality they all inhabited.

They were all getting ready for war.
The queen, their sovereign saw
that her claws she hadn't yet sunk in
to a planet not far from Sin.

Sin is the planet she took over
for she was very, very clever.
The name of her planet an outdated word
made for her a powerful sword

with which to enslave all she can
woman, child and every man.
She would want them all for her own,
this across the galaxies is widely known.
She appears only to those when
her other enemy Satan's den
is overflowing with iniquity
which it has been since antiquity.
They used to be buddies him and her
but, he did gravely err.
Taken in by her beauty, he underestimated her
strength
She, on the other hand, would go to any length
to outsmart him and lead him astray,
then to her new planet she flew away.

There she set up shop and stayed,
plans went swiftly, nothing delayed.
All her drones quickly her followed
as the old planet got emptied and hollowed
by her, and her sinister plans
to coerce, control and destroy all she can.

In working against Satan, but with the same aim
she didn't realise (as clever as she was) they played
the same game!
And although being on opposite sides it seems
there were pulling together in sordid dreams.
The two forces joined strongly as one,

the fierce war on humanity had begun.
They joined together those two forces
their reign of evil on Earth enforces
fear, anger and terror to no end
All the rules of God divine they break and bend.
They crush the precepts of the Laws of Love,
They would be in charge as a One World Gov!

These plans they hatched from many aeons before
stripping humanity of its heavenly lore
disseminating the Earthly Mother Divine.
For this, their secret evil plan they had to refine.

For the Divine Earthly Mother is wise
and from their actions she'll soon surmise
what their evil plans are.
She'd put an end to them and bar
this destruction she will try
as her weeping heart, doth cry.

Will her children heed her warning
as she shouts from the rooftops every morning
that afoot are evil plans, to destroy them all,
as they'd lost their paradise after the Fall?
Will they, her Divine wisdom heed?
They, Her help will surely need.
Some people she planted on magic soil,
that which they tilled with timeless toil.
They all got savagely murdered — dead

Their Spirits still on that sacred land tread.

Others like Earth angels delicately clad,
all full of grace and love, it's been said.
Were scattered all across the land
by mountains, forests, sea and sand
to be beacons full of love and light
and with their flame of Light blight
the darkness that'd possessed the Earth
stripped it naked of all fun and mirth.

These too were destroyed,
their minds and spirits deployed
to serve this sinister, evil plan
as Evil hi-jacked them, as it can.
For vigilant they were not,
naïvety and ignorance they had got
tricked into Evil's Illusion of light
their own Light screened off with ignorance blind.
They hadn't been clever enough to outsmart Her in
Black
and her army, which came neck-to-neck
with these Earth angels and warriors of Truth and
Light
fighting fiercely to take their light in a fight
of Good against Evil as from all Time.
She openly declared: "They are all mine."

She secretly knew

that this was not true.
For she knew the power of Light
its strength, its forceful might.
She had once been of the Light too.
But, beguiled by Satan's traps like many, not few
she fell for his illusion hook, line and sinker, so
the strength of Light she clearly did know!

Yet, her allegiance to the Beast she swore,
always black attire she wore.
Her demeanour sour, her sustenance Fear,
feeding off it wide and near.

Mary

Suddenly seemingly out of the ashes she rose
For The One in Black thought her dead, I suppose.
Alas, actually in Spirit she had been
the most beautiful Lady, the whitest you've ever
seen.
Soft, pale shining skin
to pink porcelain doll skin akin.
Draped in a silken and satin elegant, white gown
from head to the white marble floor down
hung flowing like a waterfall's pond clear and pure
matching her sweet, serene, simple demure.

She stood straight and tall facing her fairy-like, lush
garden green
with an array of colourful flower beds, butterflies
and birds as ever seen.
Fairies tended this magical piece of land
dazzling angels lent them a helping hand.
She would melt hearts with her magical, loving
smile
honest, simple, true not out to beguile.
The sun accentuated her clean compassionate heart
which she had perfected like a mesmerising piece
of art.
Not through playing evil games
or by buying into illusion's ways
as her opponent Dominic had done
hoping that that way the war'd be won.

No, Queen Mary of Heaven as many would attest,
violent manipulation, anger and fear would detest.
Yet, to understand fully her own children's plight
onto Earth she descended, alongside them to fight.
She was there in person amidst the maddening
madness
Her delicate heart breaking with so much sadness
of how far humanity had strayed,
Not in the presence of sacred Love and Light had
stayed.

She watched it all slowly unfold,
the Greatest Story still to be told.
The outcome still not made visible
to proud and evil hearts, incredible!
She suffered as she held her anguished children's hand
with Love and Compassion broken hearts she'd mend.

For their suffering was her unending pain
since the murder of her Son, she was never the same.
She had her own questions and her own brokenness too,
the same as me and the same as you.
There was a lot of healing, this is true
that Queen Mary of Heaven has had to do!

The path she chose of the meek and humble
made black clad Dominic cruelly crumble.
For Dominic couldn't understand why
this Queen so simple and sometimes shy,
gentle — sweet soft smile — all the while
would win for Heaven's side many a lost heart and mind
bringing them back to themselves and to Love, you will find.

Her orders she did not bellow and bark

she would simply pray and with a heavenly hark
entreat the sacred Conscious Power of Father-
Mother-Son
to silently and sweetly fall upon everyone.
So that this Innate Love Divine they may know
and the deep-seated peace and joy it doth bestow.
Once their hearts and minds awaken, they shine
like a heavenly choir's ecstatic music's chime
Waking up Consciousnesses that had been there,
somehow sleeping
magically dispelling the phantom-like illusion they
had been keeping,
like in a dream-like state doped
Awakening them inside, Queen Mary hoped!

Once the chime woke them up dispelling Darkness,
their Conscious awake minds would perceive the
starkness
of the bright luminous Light they now uncovered
their true identity Divine, fully awakened,
rediscovered.
For they had known all along who they had really
been,
Dominic and her troops as illusion are now being
seen.
As clear as day, it became crystal clear to all
that Dominic and her troops had procured the Fall.
Jealous of the gloriousness of Divinity in human
embodiment

Dominic and her troops fought and would not relent
to bring Humanity down into their own gruesome hell
making their embodiment a hollow sickly, sordid shell.
This of course, they couldn't really do you see,
as the Divine Conscious Spirit within, destroyed it cannot be!
So, Dominic et al had cleverly created the Illusion of it being so! Many sadly fell into this deadly delusion
and believed as they were told,
that their bodies were empty and didn't hold
the Divine Love Consciousness Supreme
manifested in and through a human being!
This suited Dominic and her troops to a tee
and in so doing, all her troops and she
would manipulate, coerce, control and destroy
all these Divine beings believing they were just a worthless toy!
It was such a clever plan
and things for Dominic were starting to pan
out — until…
the still
soft whispers of the Love inside
decided silently it will not hide
any more. It would shout out loud,
the wind of Its sound vibration moving every cloud

which each being's clear blue sky had blocked.
When this happened Dominic et al were shocked!
For the love within now fully awoken
the whispers of Truth clearly within spoken
showed beyond a shadow of a doubt
in its simple stillness, no need to shout!
That every life form of sacred Love has come
and in and through Its divine, infinite
Consciousness all this had begun.
Everywhere and every live being,
use your own minds' eyes seeing
to perceive and to see
Your own and Creations Divinity.
There is no God out here or only there,
God is in you and everywhere!
The experience of our Higher being, this *I*
is what makes us Divine and that's why
it is easy to mistake body and soul as two
when all is One, Divine Consciousness and You!

Dominic and her evil troops want us all to forget
our essential Truth, our Higher being they don't
want us to get!
For this Truth, Dominic et al are fully aware of and
know,
is what shall wake up humanity from their slumber
and show
up, all else as insidious illusion
Dominic et al all a deadly delusion,

who want to appear as truth
I think a little bit, uncouth!
It will show how as God they dressed up,
in their frenzy to deceive they wouldn't shut up.
People will perceive how hard to trick they had tried
and how through their rotten teeth to us they all lied.
Their plan to brainwash and coerce these untruths on us all
trying of Love and Light to muffle the call
Now is coming to a sudden close and soon
Dominic et al shall face their doom — BOOM!

Epilogue

It is post the Year Twenty Twenty.
Children playing everywhere a'plenty
filling up the fields and playgrounds
laughing merrily on the merry-go-rounds
relishing ice-cream cups and cones by the score
happily sliding down slippery slides, galore!
Swinging high up in the air
shrieks of laughter everywhere.
Children joyfully playing in groups
from near and from afar like troops
who are celebrating their victory
over years of treacherous tyranny!

Most adult-like beings had stayed sadly asleep.
The children knew that *they* Life must keep
going, and living according to their own Light
fighting for freedom with all their might.
To begin with it had been very hard
not a glimmer of hope, not a shard.
Yet amongst them a child-like grown up said:
"This is wrong DO NOT CONSENT, you must rise
up instead!
You must not stay in your bubble or square
be the day rainy or be it fair.
You must NOT keep two metres apart
not the size of a bus, nor the size of a cart!

You must look at each other with wonder and care
you must have great courage and you must dare
to go against these evil edicts that stop
your freedom, and your Life-Force crop!"

The *children and other child-like adults* listened
intently to this
seeing that their own families and friends they all
do miss,
decided to heed this child-like woman's call
put an end to this tyranny, once and for all!

The children sadly saw their parents are still fast
asleep
and knew that *they* the light a'glowing must keep.
Life was disappearing fast from the planet, oh so
fast,
they must act quickly, before the last
remnants of uncontaminated air disappeared
and the Earth of pure air is deliberately cleared.
The *children* knew that deep, deep inside
the little voice which inside likes to hide
Echoed the words of this child-like woman with
hair
that made her look like a big brown grisly bear!
Yet, her heart kind like that made of gold,
in all fairness, this must be told!
They all began to pull together as One

To save Humanity *their* mission had begun!
'Twasn't 'Save the Children' campaign — it was not.
It was the other way around, as the *children* had got
what it takes to set enslaved grown-ups free
and so it was '*Children* Save Humanity', you see!

They summoned their courage like a loud lion's roar
as how Humanity needs them, *they* very clearly saw.
Their parents fast asleep, needed waking up soon
otherwise *everybody* would be facing their doom.
In their bubbles they decided they would not stay
face the consequences they would, come what may!
They would not stand two metres apart
"What good would that do?" they asked for a start.
These were *children and child-like adults who*
urgently needed to play
needed to hug, dance, skip and jump in abandon
without further delay.
Although in many these urges had been wiped out
there were still enough Voices who started to shout:

"All you adult-like beings, all you out there, you

should all be ashamed
at how controlled, fearful and gullible you are,
you've ALL been framed!
These measures to keep you so much further apart
edicts that from Freedom, Life and Love depart.
These measures to wear a mask on your face
a symbol of slavery on your face you embrace.
The vaccine, part and parcel of the plot and the ploy
dehumanising your being like an artificial plastic toy.
The nano tech that is imparted within it
will your mind and body control and inhabit.
In the end you wouldn't know whether you're coming or going
this is the end of all your seeing, hearing, feeling and knowing!

We *children* from across the world united in Will shall be
as this predicament of you sheep-walking adults we see.
You are doped up on sugar and sickly sweets,
eating junk food and gorging forbidden meats.
Innocent animals being murdered for your whims
these are on you — their deaths — your sins!
We the *children* are eating well and very healthily
as how you've ruined your health we so readily see.

We the *children* shall save *your* lives
Outside the hexagon of your bee hives
that have been built to enslave each and every one
We shall step out of it now, your liberation's
begun!

We are awake and for goodness' sake
have come you all free to make
Free from the tyranny of slavery.
Admire our bravado and bravery
and join us unanimously
As we fight forcefully, tirelessly
to cut these fierce fetters that bind
procuring for you Freedom and Life of soul, body
and mind."
So like the pied-piper of Hamlyn the Woman
played her flute.
The *children's* voices who followed her were loud,
not mute.
They could be heard from east to west
and north to south as all would attest
to hearing their voices loud and clear
whether relatively far, or whether quite near.
They danced, skipped and jumped whilst they
sang
as their Voices throughout the Earth's ends rang.

They reverberated throughout workplaces, offices
and schools

through playgrounds, shops and outdoor pools.
Their singing was incessant and did not stop
heard in every street corner and corner shop.
Some dressed in white and others in blue
they came to wake me up, and yes You!
A *child's* gentle call waking you up from your slumber
gently nudging you and hoping you remember
that you need NOT BE AFRAID
nor into a subservient slave made.
And if this gentle nudge is not enough
then *children* are made of tougher stuff
and would form choirs of different symphonies
waking up your minds, souls and dormant bodies.
They were not going to give up and cease
all in the name of a non-existent, made up 'deadly' disease!

A fear of death children have got none
although some adults sadly in some
did put the fear of Death into their offspring
their bodies alive, silently and lifelessly sing
the song of the wretched Reaper
scared to death, that as their Keeper
He will come suddenly to gather their 'sinful' soul
fear and fear of death these deluded parents' goal.
Sadly, passing on fear ignited by Church State
many adult-like parents to this did relate.
The fear spread from parent to daughter or son

like wildfire it spread almost to everyone!

Some *children* were spared and what a relief
as their power to fight had been beyond belief.
These are the ones following the Woman
there is one thing they all had in common,
The innermost voice within hadn't been muffled
their minds and their mouths hadn't been muzzled.
Mostly thanks to child-like grown-ups who, an
open mind had kept
and in the chaotic, confusing current state of
affairs had not slept.
But tirelessly and ceaselessly worked to awaken
at great personal expense — do not be mistaken
for easy it had not been —
but worth it as we have seen!

For these *children* entrusted to Save Humanity
now
altogether in the playing fields gathered somehow.
It is thanks to *them* that evil regimes suddenly fell
joyful knell, after joyful knell of a peaceful bell
heralding Freedom, Justice, Life and *their* Victory
How it all happened, the greatest Mystcry.

Fetters falling
Voices calling
Bars breaking
Earth's quaking

157

Cells disseminating
Spirits rejuvenating

Finally, Evil melts into obsidian oblivion.
Freedom, Life and Love rule, No Division!
A child-like being, its faith and power triumphant
over all
What would we've done hadn't our *children*
heeded the call?
What fearful Fate would Humanity had faced
had *her children* their headstrong heads not
raised?
What would have become of her sleep-walking
sheep,
hadn't it had *children* a watchful eye on Truth to
keep?
What would've happened had these *children* been
had too
and wouldn't have been able to wake up me and
you?
What if these *children* hadn't heeded the call
deeming they were insignificant, too small?
What if the last shreds of Life in *them* had been
destroyed
and their Life-Force to this aim had not been
deployed?
Luckily for us all — these *children* saved
Humanity

from enslavement, imprisonment, death and
tyranny.

Divinity in a human embodiment ethereally veiled
its Word, through child-like Beings readily
revealed.
Out of the mouth of innocent babes,
adult-like beings awoken in waves!
A Voice is never too small
to proclaim the message to all.
Waking up sleeping adult-like beings Divine
who live and act like hellish beasts who dine
on egos and illusions far too big to care to see
their broken, fallen Humanity
having lost all its dignity.
All must heal
Its division
Free it from its prison
Uncover the lies
Answer the 'whys'
Question the State
Before it's too late!

But fully awake they are now
saved by their children, somehow!
Truth within them opens its eyes,
Life, Love, Light, like the phoenix, rise!

Printed in Great Britain
by Amazon